If You Should See Me Walking on the Road

For Grace —
No, I do not have
an orange face!

If You Should See Me Walking on the Road

Poems by

J.R. Solonche

Cover design by Shay Culligan

ISBN: 978-1-950462-01-8

Kelsay Books Inc.

kelsaybooks.com

502 S 1040 E, A119
American Fork, Utah 84003

Books by J.R. Solonche

Peach Girl: Poems for a Chinese Daughter
    (with Joan I. Siegel)
Beautiful Day
Heart's Content (chapbook)
Won't Be Long
The Black Birch
Invisible
In Short Order
I, Emily Dickinson & Other Found Poems
Tomorrow, Today and Yesterday
True Enough

Acknowledgments

Allegro Poetry Review: "Anniversary"

Brasilia Review: "Twilight"

Centaur: "The Meadow"

Chronogram: "Dialogue with a Dead Beaver" "Hamlet Haiku"

Milo Review: "On Being Asked by a Child to Teach Her How to Tell Time"

Offcourse: A Literary Journal: "New Journey"

One Sentence Poems: "Law & Order"

Poet & Critic: "Terra Cotta"

Poetry Storehouse: "Ah! What Right" "Crows Again"

Review Americana: "Desk"

Salmon Poetry: Dogs Singing, A Tribute Anthology: "My Dog"

The Lake: "Afterglow"

Contents

If You Should See Me Walking on the Road

If you should see me walking on the road
alone in the rain, without coat or covering,
my hair matted, the rain running like long
slender plaits of silver hair down my neck,
my shoulders, and I am not smiling, do not
be concerned. Do not worry, for I will know
where I am, and I will know where I am going.
But if you should see me walking on the road
alone in the rain, without coat or covering,
my hair matted, the rain running like long
slender plaits of silver hair down my neck,
my shoulders, and I am smiling, be concerned.
There will be reason to worry, for I will not know
where I am, and I will not know where I am going.

Dog in a Car with Alaska Plates

Boy, you're about as far from home
as you can be, aren't you?
But you're used to waiting there,
in the back seat. I can see that.
You look at me through the half-open
window just the same way you've looked
at hundreds before me, just the same way
you'll look at hundreds more. Boy,
you have calm eyes, just about the calmest
I've ever seen, in dog or man.
And the emptiest. So empty, they're full.
Are you homesick? You look right at home
in that car, I can't believe you're homesick,
but you miss Alaska, don't you boy?
I can tell. I can see it in your calm eyes.
In your empty full eyes. In your full empty eyes.

The Night Is Warm

The night is warm.

I walk along the lake road.

In the distance, a dog has begun to bark.

It sounds like the slap of a hand against the dark.

In the middle of the lake, the geese stir.

They cry out and shake their wings.

Such a big family.

I envy them that.

It is almost time to settle down for the night.

There is a light at the far end of the lake.

The doctor must be home.

Soon I will be home.

I have very little time.

I must remind myself of everything I know.

There are only two things I know.

Therefore I will not need very much time.

Life has a beginning, a middle, and an end.

Death has a beginning, and no middle, and no end.

In the distance the dog has stopped.

The deer must be out of sight.

In the middle of the lake, the geese are quiet.

They have settled down for the night.

At the far end of the lake, the light burns.

The doctor is still awake.

Hawks

My neighbors are red-shouldered hawks.
They have an aerie in the woods behind the house.
I hear them whistle to each other in the morning,
and the late afternoon or early evening.
Sometimes I catch a glimpse of one severing
the space over the road between tree canopies,
like a bullet in slow-motion. Or splitting
the heavy log of summer air into kindling.
This morning I saw the female on my lawn
dismembering her prey with her beak and talons.
She must have known it was my ground,
for she ate with small, polite, even dainty bites,
all the while with her back to me.

So the Student Who Wanted to Be a Poet

So the student who wanted to be a poet
asked the Zen master,
"Master, what should I do when I cannot write?"
"When you cannot write,"
answered the Zen master, "do not write."

Nothing Is Older

Nothing is older
than an old poem.
No ancient river,
no ancient stone,
no ancient mountain
is more ancient than
an old poem. No old
girlfriend, no old pair
of shoes, no old pocket
watch is older than
an old poem.

Conjectures of Emily

She was plain, a spinster
who lived alone in
her father's house. Her
favorite word was "death."

In secret, she knew
a glorious garden where
guarded poems grew
up tall and straight.

What she did not say,
she did not know.
She had to hold, day
after day, the world

in one hand, her heart
in the other, arms
stretched apart
until they balanced.

In secret, she very well
knew a poem from a heart.
A poem is unbreakable.
Broken cups, too, she kept.

Something about Snow

Something about snow despises noise.
I mean something other than vast white sound-

proofing in the walls and ceiling of the world.
Something more subtle than that about snow

despises noise, for even the loudest, the most
oafish of males on campus are quiet today.

Oh, snow, White Knight of silence,
bringer of civilization, I thank you.

Terra Cotta

It is the same every year.

October ends, November begins,

December stirs like a gray flower on the horizon.

The impatiens, flowering white, pink, red, orange,

flourishing half a year since May,

killed overnight by the killing frost,

are pulled by the roots from the terra cotta pots,

dumped on the leaves of the pin oaks and the ashes.

The soil scraped out of the pots,

the pots rinsed, lined up to dry on the stone wall,

stored in the shed until the spring.

Except each year a pot is cracked and needs

to be replaced.

Except each year you look more closely

at the dead plants, at the living dirt.

Sunflowers

Tall as a man,
tall as I am,
but thin
like men who
have fasted
in the desert
forty days
and forty nights,
your heads
are bowed,
but the sun
is haloed
around
your heads,
as men
who have seen
visions in
the desert
return hallowed
to the world
of men.
Sunflowers,
to the flowers,

trees,

to the flowers,

gods,

face-to-face

with me,

let me prove

something

to myself,

let me shake

your shoulders,

let me make

you listen,

let me see

you quake

in your boots,

from your roots,

for their sake.

Song

I have always wanted
(at least ever since
reading Creeley)
to write a poem called "Song."
Hey, nonny nonny.

For Giants, Sound and Fury Mean Nothing
(Sports Headline)

Don't get me wrong.

We are not hard of hearing.

In fact, our hearing is very acute.

Just look at these ears the size of trashcan lids.

No, it's just that we giants

are not bothered by your sound and fury.

Our heads are in the clouds.

We are above it all.

The boasting and the bombast

of you little ones down there,

you who yelp like Yorkies at our heels,

who rap your knuckles on our ankles.

No, your sound and fury

mean nothing to us.

They are less than the names

you call us that will never hurt.

Less than the sticks and stones

that you try to use to break our bones,

but will likewise never hurt.

Less even than twigs and pebbles

that do not do so much as break

our concentration much less our bones.

No, sound and fury are for you down there.

For midgets, sound and fury mean everything.

Four Geese on the Lawn of the Elementary School

How long have they been here I wonder
on the lawn of the elementary school,

the grass not yet cut, still thick and sweet,
and the dandelions still bright yellow and still

spread out around them like their own golden eggs?
It looks like they've been here all morning.

It looks like they've been arguing all morning.
It looks like they have just now agreed

while one, only reluctantly persuaded,
now waddles away from the other three,

still, in her heart, unpersuaded, still, in
her heart, not yet ready to teach us their secret.

Island Ghazal

On the beach are stones of every color in the world.
The breakers that broke them are the ego of the island.

Look at your footprints, one in front of the other.
Each is a wink of lake, a negative island.

You are the stranger in the strangers' photograph.
You are the one gazing out from her own island.

You hear the wind, the surf, the gulls.
Your eyes are closed on every island.

A lone cormorant dives in the ocean swells.
It says, "What an island!"

Now it is night and the moon rises.
It is the chrome plated cliché of an island.

So, Solonche, why do you lie awake staring at the moon?
"Why? To remember that all that exists are islands."

Last Peony

I couldn't resist picking it,

as I could not resist picking the first.

Bringing it in, putting it in a vase,

like fitting a new candle to a holder.

The last peony in the garden,

round, pink on pink on pink, still

opening one upon the other,

among a dozen spent peonies,

each as dark as a burnt match head

the wind has blown out

before the summer can catch.

My Dog

So many people with dogs in the park today,
it makes me wonder what kind of dog
I would have if I had a dog. I never had a dog.
When I was five, I was chased by a dog.
I think it was a bull terrier. It looked like the dog
on the old *Our Gang* comedies, but without
the black ring around its eye. It chased me
into the alley behind the apartment building.
I climbed up onto one of the iron bars
that connected the iron railing to the wall.
The dog kept barking as I kept my balance
as best I could, but I was five, and I lost it
and fell off and split my nose open.
Maybe this is why I never had a dog.
There's one I like, a big black one.
The one that looks like a bear.
The one with the big brown doleful eyes.
The one that looks like the only reason
he gets off the couch is to go out to take a crap.
The one whose master is pulling hard on the leash
to get to cross the street into the park.

Tag

This morning, playing tag with a friend,
my daughter says, *Daddy, stand there*
without moving. Pretend you're a tree.
So I pretend to be a tree. I stand in one
spot without moving, except for my arms,
which are my branches moving in the wind.
Because she does not specify the kind of tree,
I choose my favorite, the wild cherry tree.
I close my eyes and pretend with all
my might to be a wild cherry tree. I turn
my feet into roots, thrusting them downward
into the earth. My toes grow to root tips,
worming through the soil. I dig my place.
I turn my body into trunk, my bones
into wood, my heart into heartwood,
my blood into tree sap, my skin into bark.
I turn my hair into leaves, or rather the buds
of leaves for it is only March. I empty
my mind of all untree-like thoughts, which
is to say I think of nothing but rain
and birds' nests and bees. I empty my heart
of all untree-like desires, which is to say I feel

no desire but the desire to flower and seed.

I pretend to be a wild cherry tree so well

that when my daughter's game is over

and she taps my shoulder and says, *Daddy,*

you can stop being a tree now, I don't want

to stop being a wild cherry tree. I don't want

to start thinking untree-like thoughts.

I don't want to start feeling untree-like desires.

I smile and ask, *So, was I a good tree?*

My daughter doesn't answer. She is already

off playing a game that doesn't require a tree.

Advice

"Live in the moment,"
my mother told me,
so I lived in the moment.

"Live for the moment,"
my father told me,
so I lived for the moment.

"Live at the moment,"
my grandfather told me,
so I lived at the moment.

"Live around the moment,"
my grandmother told me,
so I lived around the moment.

"Live with the moment,"
my uncle told me,
so I lived with the moment.

"Live about the moment,"
my aunt told me,
so I lived about the moment.

"Live by the moment,"
my girlfriend told me,
so I lived by the moment.

"Live during the moment,"
the bartender told me,
so I lived during the moment.

"Live along the moment,"
my lawyer told me,
so I lived along the moment.

I was confused,
so I read a book
by a famous Zen master.

"Live without prepositions,"
he told me,
so I live the moment.

The Woman's Is the Better Body

The woman's is the better body.
The man's is the worse.

The woman's body is all four corners of the world.
The man's body is one.

The best the man's body can do
is point to the woman's body.

The most the soul of the man's body can do is say,
"Here is the body I want to be in."

January

The lake is frozen.
It is ice, and it has snowed, so now the lake,
which is a sheet of ice, is under a blanket of snow.

The wind has died down.
It is still, and the stillness is the ghost of the wind.
Two geese fly over the lake.

Their cries echo upon the snow covered ice.
Then they are gone.
Then their cries are gone.

Then the echo is gone.
Then it is still again.
The lake is alone.

Twilight

Twilight, and the light follows the sound of a plane west.
The sound fades away, and the light fades after it.
It is pulled, unwilling to leave, and it turns while leaving.
All there is to hear is the water and the birds.

But the sound of the water is not the voice of the water only.
On the tongue of the water is also the voice of the culvert.
And the sound of the birds is not the sound of the birds only.
In the mouths of the birds is also the voice of the empty road.

Afterglow

I asked the poet what her poem
was about because at first I thought
it was about sex, and then I thought
it was about a nuclear war, and then
I thought it was about sex again.
I thought it was about sex because
of the lightning and the tides ebbing
and flowing and the crater and, of
course, because of the title, "Afterglow,"
but then I changed my mind and thought
it was about a nuclear war because of
the lightning and the tides ebbing and
flowing and the crater and especially
because the stuff that filled the crater
was green which I took to be new grass
growing after the nuclear war and semen
is yellow, not green, and because of
the title, "Afterglow," and I changed my
mind and thought it was really about
sex after all because of the ending
with its Ah and Oh, aftermath and afterglow,
which so reminded me of the lovely light
of Edna Millay's both-ends-burning candle,

which is about sex. So I asked the poet
what her poem was about, and she stared
at me and said, "It's self-evident," and
I said, "You're right. It is. How stupid
of me to ask," and she stared at me and said,
"That, too, is self-evident," and she turned
away to talk to someone else, and I was left
there in the corner, alone in the afterglow
of the sex of our nuclear war.

Country Cemetery

Snow, vast white shadow
on the buried
stones. On the iron
fence around three sides.

The fourth side spills into
the trees. The fence
is bent there to buried.
A blur of briars.

I imagine their ages,
not seeing their ages.
The dead and buried
that I am standing on.

Their stones are falling
too slowly to see.
Each stone is closing
like a mind long buried

in secret thoughts.

They too wish to sleep.

Grain by grain.

To sleep buried

in the earth,

amidst the trees,

they too long for it.

Buried anonymity.

Porsche

At twilight on the county road,
I found myself behind a beautiful Porsche.

It was a model from the sixties.
It was white. And, as I say,

it was beautiful. It turned onto the road
that leads to the road that leads to my house.

I followed it as far as the road to my house.
Then, as I turned off, I watched it disappear

in the dimming dusk. It looked like the ghost
of a red Porsche haunting the road

on which it had been killed.
It looked like the half-moon slumming

down here in earth's earthy neighborhood.
It was the car Ezra Pound would have designed

had Ezra Pound been a car designer.
Use no unnecessary metal, said its exhaust.

Funeral

It was all a lie. And we knew it.
She wasn't kind. She wasn't loving.
She wasn't an inspiration. But we
didn't care. It didn't matter. What
would have been gained by saying
she was an angry woman, that she
was full of hate, that she was hard
and cold, that all she inspired in
her daughters was fear and icy
disappointment? Perhaps we would
have felt a momentary satisfaction.
A bitter smile might have passed
over our lips, but the guilt would
have followed, stronger than ever,
touching even this, casting its shadow,
longer than ever, reaching even here.
They were lies, but they tasted good.
They satisfied. The human heart lives
on them. They are its bread.

Ambition

Someday I will write a love poem
in which the word love does not appear,
just as someday I will write a poem about death
in which the word death is not mentioned.
Once I accomplish this, I will be ready to go on
to the much more difficult and write a love poem
mentioning the word love, and write a poem
about death with the word death.

Wheels

In the outpatient waiting area, I wait.
Wheelchairs, wheelchairs are everywhere.
Wheelchairs if not with people in them,

then wheelchairs empty and waiting.
Everyone is my grandmother.
Everyone is my grandfather.

Everyone is my other grandmother.
Everyone is my other grandfather.
Now I remember my mother saying,

"No roller skates for my son."
Now I remember my mother saying,
"No tricycle for my son."

Now I remember my mother saying,
"No bicycle for my son."
Now I remember my mother saying,

"No soapbox racer for my son."
Now I know why my mother said,
"No wheels, nothing with wheels for my son."

Anniversary

We talked of what years do to us.
It was a fairly average day.
We made love with old, familiar lust.

We put our daughter on the bus.
We said the things we had to say.
We talked of what years do to us.

We had appointments at the dentist,
for cleaning and for x-ray.
We made love with old, familiar lust.

No one called. No one made a fuss.
The January sky was gray.
We talked of what years do to us.

You returned a nightgown, Christmas
gift too big. It was on the way.
We made love with old, familiar lust.

Did we kiss? I think we did kiss.

But anyway... So anyway...

We talked of what years do to us

and made love with old, familiar lust.

On Being Asked by a Child to Teach Her How to Tell Time

Well, I really don't think I should teach you how to tell time. It's against my better judgment. But if I don't teach you, someone else will, just as someone else taught you how to spell C-A-T and how to get 4 by adding 2 and 2 and how to drink from a glass without spilling, so I guess I will teach you how to tell time even though it's such a foolish thing to learn. How to tell time is reading a clock for some kinds of time and reading a calendar for other kinds of time. This is confusing because there is only one kind of time, which also is confusing because there are really no kinds of time at all. Anyway, it is all just adding and subtracting. (Remember 2 and 2 is 4?) But at some time in the future, you will discover for yourself that it is all subtracting and no adding. How to tell time by a clock is looking at the big had and the little hand. They are two foreigners, one tall one short, who don't speak English. They are standing at the fork in a road in a country you are visiting but whose language you don't understand. You want to know where you are and which way to go, so you ask directions. The tall one points one way. The short one points another way. Sometimes they both point the same way. However, they agree for only a minute, and then they point different ways again. Anyway, this doesn't matter. At some point on your journey through this foreign country, you will find out for yourself that there is no fork in the road and no road and no country. How to tell time by calendar is much easier. It's the same as reading a book with only 19 words. Sometimes there are other words, but they are always the names of holidays. You make up the story as you turn the pages. The problem is the faster you turn them, the shorter the story becomes. But that doesn't matter. Just be careful not to turn to the last page to see what happens at the end. Well, I guess that doesn't matter either. The last page is always the same. There. I've taught you how to tell time. And I'm very sorry for it. I should have taught you something else. I should have taught you *what* to tell time. I should have taught you, for instance, to tell time this: You know him for what he is, a liar, a braggart, and a boor. And that he doesn't have to wear a smile for you or you for him. And I should have taught you to tell time "Thank you" for whatever he gives you, but that you cannot give him much of your time, not even the time of day, because you're too busy to pass the time with him. And although he's been around for so long, he's not much wiser for it. There are lots of other things I wish I had taught you to tell time, but he's very impatient (as I see you are getting to be) and his attention span is quite limited. But I'm most sorry that I didn't teach you to tell time this: That you learned this from me, whom you knew just as briefly.

The Meadow

The small pond nearly dry.

The stream also empty.

The rain last night

and the drizzle this morning

hardly enough

to break the drought.

One horse in the meadow.

I remember his two companions.

I watch him.

He is strong and graceful.

His companions

are strong and graceful on either side.

He is alone, eating.

The tail waves.

Theirs wave.

Three waves.

Now he looks up.

The neck is a tree.

The eyes are large and dark.

They look up.

Their necks are trees.

Their eyes are large and dark.

I want his eyes to ask

about his companions.

But no.

They say: "See.

All this hay is mine."

Apology to the Reader

I admit it. I have not written a good poem,
and I apologize. There is no excuse.
It should have been good but it wasn't.
I wrote it the first thing this morning, before
breakfast. That was a mistake. I have never
written a good poem on an empty stomach.
I shouldn't have tried. Also, I had to use
an unfamiliar pen. My favorite fine felt-tipped
pen ran out of ink last week and I forgot
to buy a refill, so I had to use a cheap Bic.
The heft was wrong and it kept slipping
out of my hand. Another thing you should
know. I couldn't find the yellow legal pad
I always write good poems on, so I wrote
it on whatever was at hand, one of my
daughter's extra sixth grade composition
books. Even Robert Frost couldn't have
written anything decent on that paper.
Anyway, I'm sorry that I have not written
a good poem. I'll make it up to you. I'll write
two tomorrow. After breakfast. I promise.

Wastepaper Basket

Sometimes you are a giant ear
eavesdropping on my life,
a cynic, filled only with failure.

Sometimes you are an enormous
mouth locked open, hungry as a baby owl,
petulant, mocking my muteness.

Sometimes you are a well gone dry,
in a desert, filling up with sand,
or the beginning of my grave,

empty by three shovels
before the shovel squares you,
then makes you my size.

Desk

1.

The desk is a desert.
But where else can I plant
the white flowers?

2.

The desk, the paper, the pen.
These three inseparable brothers.
They even sleep together.

3.

Old man White Paper is my guest.
He must not leave without
finishing the black wine.

4.

The desk is getting old.
Everyday there are more and more
wrinkles on her face.

5.

The white paper is the door
I have cut in the wall of the desk.
When my pen taps, who will open it to let me in?

6.

The desk is my palomino,
the paper my saddle, the pen my whip.
No, this is cruel.

7.

Tonight the desk
is nothing but my elbows'
hard wooden bed.

To My Desk Chair

Thank you for
putting me
in my place.

Skunk

Six times I passed the dead skunk on the road.

Six times I thought the same black thoughts.

Six times I thought the same white thoughts.

Six times I felt the breeze through the window.

Six times I wondered what you were doing.

Six times I noticed the reddening of the maples.

Six times I smelled the black smell of skunk.

Six times I smelled the white smell of skunk.

Six times I remembered where I was going.

Six times I decided on cremation.

Six times I turned up the volume of the radio.

Six times I glanced up to see the storm clouds.

Six times I reminded myself sixty-one really is not old.

Six times I cursed my stupidity for wasting gas.

Six times I remembered the first line of that poem by Lowell.

Six times I wondered if the crows would be first.

Six times I wondered if the vultures would be first.

Six times I scratched the back of my hand.

Six times I said the word *skunk* six times.

We Met on Campus

I didn't recognize him.
He had a full beard.
"It looks great," I said.
"I like it." "It's my
retirement beard," he
said. "Thirty-five days
to go." "It really looks
great," I said. "I really
like it. I want to let
mine grow someday."
But what day? The day
I turn sixty-five? The day
my old Norelco dies?
The day the Dodgers win
the pennant? The day
my daughter gets married?
The day I become a grandfather?
The day the age of vanity
becomes the vanity of age?
Yes, that's the day, the
day the age of vanity
becomes the vanity of age.

In the Meeting

When the Chair told us
not to worry about
the new policy because
the VP for Academic
Affairs said it wasn't cast
in concrete but was "written
in sand," Jim said, "Yeah,
but don't forget that sand
is an ingredient in concrete."

The Last Thoughts of King Hamlet

Ahhhh… sex with Gertrude in the afternoon.
I always sleep well after doggie style.
What an ass that woman has. What an ass
that pipsqueak Fortinbras is. Wants revenge,
does he? Took me almost an hour to kill
the elder one. The son I'll slay in no
time flat. I'm twice his age and twice the man
he'll ever be. My Danes will mow them down,
those dumb Norwegians. Say, I wonder what
he's up to at that university
of his, my son. What's it called? Wittenbug?
Or Mittenberg? Or Bittenmug? I hear
the girls in Germany are uglier
than sin. Ha, ha, ha. Poor Hamlet. Too bad.
That girlfriend here in Elsinore, now there's
a pretty one. Oh, what's her name again?
Felicia… Felicity… Oh… feel… ahzzzzzz.

Intimations of Intimation

The sky is blue.
The air is clear and cold.
The red tails are whistling across the lake.

I have the feeling that if I stand out here
long enough I will have the feeling
some great truth will make itself known to me.

It will not be the blue truth of the sky,
although it will also be that.
It will not be the clear cold truth of the air,

although it will also be that.
It will not be the whistling truth of the red tails
across the lake, although it will also be that.

It will be more than that,
this great truth I have a feeling
I will have a feeling about if I stand out here long enough.

It will be more than
these intimations of intimation,
more than this pale imitation of imitation.

Hopper: 7 A.M. 1948

The edge of the building
marks the end of the town,

the edge of the woods.
A store. But what kind?

The bottles in the window.
Beer or hair tonic?

And the advertisements.
What are they advertising?

The center is the clock.
And the clock is the center.

And its shadow is the center.
And time and its shadow.

Friday

i

How many words here,
in this three-inch yellow chalk?
Hundreds. Thousands. Where?

ii.

In the stall, a turd,
stinking in stinking urine.
The stinking bastard.

iii

To me (in mirror):
Like William, see double, you!
From me. (In mirror.)

iv

I bring to my lips
this fourth cup of black coffee.
But not in friendship.

v

Going out, he said,
Fridays are so beautiful!
Always are, the dead.

vi

What? A hummingbird
up here in February?
Sun on green light. Red.

vii

"No doubt accomplished.
Still we're returning this batch.
They're not what we wished."

Very Short Dialogue

He: So, what are my shortcomings?

She: Your short comings.

The Fog in the Valley

The fog in the valley is heavy.
It covers the farms.
It will never lift from the silos, the barns,
the farmhouses.

The fog in the valley is heavy
and will never rise
from the horses, the cow, the pig, the geese,
the children.

The dogs bark through the fog.
The cows and the infants cry through it.
The lighted windows of the farmhouses
cry through the heavy fog

that will never clear from them,
barely visible and yellow so long,
the people of the valley believe it is their breath.

Days

It has been days,
and after days,
a man becomes
his mood, and
after days the flesh
forgets, and days
doom the body
to witnessing.

The Birth of Venus

"See," they say, "we
have come to make,
with our own breath,
a beautiful breeze
to move you on your
shell to shore."

"See," she says, "I
have come to meet
you, to give you, as
you step from your
shell onto shore,
a silken shift."

"Why have I come?"
she asks.

April

Now I lack
nothing,
for I lie here
in the sun,
inhaling the lilac.

Student Recital

Twenty-two
played the piano.

Two played
music.

Holy Shit

Galway Kinnell's "Holy Shit"
is the kind of poem
that gives poetry a bad name.

My New Neighbor

introduces herself
as "Pat the Former Nun."

Force of habit
no doubt.

A Portrait of the Artist

He looks
as if he
is gazing out

a window
or walking
through a door.

Mind you,
this is
all the time.

Apple Orchard in Early March

Here is the cemetery

of the 1000 soldiers

who fought and died

for their country

whose religion

was Knowledge,

whose deity was Eve.

Christmas

The first house has a giant
inflatable snowman on
the front lawn. It waves
an inflatable candy cane.
I wave my inflatable arm.
The second house has two
electrified deer. One nods
its head up and down, *Yes.*
The other shakes its head
from side to side, *No.*
I nod my electrified head,
Yes, yes. I shake it, *No, no.*
The third house is dark.
There are no snowmen.
There are no deer. There
is no Santa in his sleigh.
There are no lights, only
a wreath on the front door.
The porch frowns at me.
I turn dark. I weave a wreath
around my face. I frown.
Hey, it's Christmas.
One must be agreeable.

Daffodils

How do we know
they are not really
brave, these yellow
daffodils, keeping
their heads up as
best they can against
the cold wind of this
unseasonable April,
or as we say,
Braving the elements?

Peonies

How does it do it,
bring one peony to flower

while the others stay knotted,
then, as the flowering peony's petals fall,

untie, one by one, the others?
How does it do it, all this opening

and closing simultaneously,
without going stark raving mad?

Poets

Nietzsche had it wrong
when he said, "I don't like
poets: They lie." Didn't
he realize that's the only
reason one should like poets,
the way they charm your socks
off while lying to your face?

Religion

So let us believe that the rain
needs the lilac as much as
the lilac needs the rain.
Why not? What harm can it do
other than to be mistaken?

The Surfaces

Cut through the world,
and you reveal the surfaces
of the inner world. Cut through
that, and you reveal more surfaces.
As long as there are eyes to see,
there are surfaces to be seen.
This is why blindness is so
closely associated with wisdom.

Dialogue with a Dead Beaver

I did not know what you were
in the tall weeds until I saw
the incisors in your jaw and what
remained of your paddle of tail.
Black, all black, even your bones.
In my weeds by the road I am black.
I wanted to believe that a hundred
yards down the road from the spot
where you were hit, a car swerved
straight into a deep ditch,
felled by a gash in one of the tires.
You want to believe I kill what kills me.
I wanted to say that your smell
was the smell of rich, black earth
from which a miraculous tree
would grow someday, a tree that
would grow again and again
endlessly as it was endlessly felled.
My smell is black. My flies are black.

Winter

Snow, snow, snow, snow, snow, snow, snow, so now,
so, now I am drinking red wine and reading the calendar.

The calendar was not written by a poet.
The calendar was not written by a lover of red wine.

Poets should not write poetry only.
They should write the news.

They should write the weather and the sports.
They should write the warning on the cigarette packages.

They should write the user manuals for the automobiles.
They should write the dictionaries.

They should write the constitutions for
the new democracies.

They should write the briefs for the lawyers
and the decisions of the judges.

They should write the economics textbooks.
They should write the math textbooks.

They should write the self-help books.
They should write the travel books.

They should write the cookbooks.
They should write the comic books.

They should write the speeches for the politicians.
They should write the labels for the red wine bottles.

They should write the calendars.
Especially the calendars.

The poets should write everything.
And the lovers of red wine should rule the world.

Perspective

When the body
is very quiet and
very still, the mind,
which has very patiently
been waiting, speaks up.
This is called dreaming by some.

White Lilac in May

If sheep grew on trees,
this is how they are born,
these embryonic cones
of white wool.

Frost

The grass this morning
is covered with frost,
gone white overnight,
frightened to death
by winter's cold steel.

Blackbird

The woman who owned
the motel said the blackbird
followed me in the parking lot
because "you have a great soul."
The day I believe that is the day
I commit suicide without leaving a note.

Index

Twenty-four pages.
All there is after
thirty years of it.

Geese

Visible through the trees, two
vees of geese heading
west by northwest, parallel, until one
veers toward the other, then separates and
vanishes. And vanishes.

Napkin

"You're the most beautiful
woman I've ever seen,"
I wrote on a napkin, and
I meant it, I meant it
at the time, and gave it
to her, but she didn't bat an eye.

Well Then

Well then if I have to sit
here for all this time and do
nothing except look out the window
at the rain, that is what I'll do.
I will not go mad. I will not gain wisdom.
But when I'm done, I will know more
about sitting, and I will know more
about looking, and I will know more about rain.

Crows Again

I had almost forgotten
just how big crows are
until four came down
to the feeder where
the juncos and titmice
made way. Each one
easily the size of six
of them, the only thing
missing was *Hell's Angels*
in white across their broad,
blacker than motorcycle-
black-leather jacket backs.

Ah! What Right

has the sky to be
so beautiful today?
With its clouds
just the right round
and just the right
white in just
the right corner
with just the right
hawks whistling
just the right
whistles against
just the right sunlight?

When I Showed the Class

two poems on the same theme,
one by Dickinson and one by Frost
and said, "If the tone of a poem
is its weather, what would you
say about the weather of these?"
"The Dickinson is clear.
The Frost is a darker kind of clear,"
someone answered.

An Old Mirror

Here is the one for the old,
this antique mirror that has gone
blind from lifetimes of staring
into the light. Here, this is the one
to take them into its soft glass
arms, to keep them, the old,
and sing them to sleep.

Whatever Possessed that Woman

that Ruth Lily, who was once
rejected by *Poetry,* to decide
to bequeath that magazine
$100, 000,000? What the hell
did she expect them to do with it?
Didn't she know money corrupts
and absolute money corrupts absolutely?

Great Blue Heron

Here is the hero,
this heron, in blue
disdain of our dance
of life, rising from
the marsh to weigh
the world and find
it wanting.

Law & Order

The only way
to stop a bad poet
with a pen
is a good poet
with a gun.

.

Someone

added an erect
phallus to the six-
point buck on the deer
crossing sign.
The same ass-hole,
no doubt, who changed
the three to an eight
on the 30 MPH sign.

The Waves

The waves
on the lake
are the wind
if the wind
were the water.

The Woman

opening the overhead
to get something
from her bag,
said to the man
directly below, "I'll
try not to drop it
on your head."
"It's all right. I'm
a Jewish lawyer," he said.

Train

Have you noticed
that people are never
more private than
when in public?

A Solitary Hawk

A solitary hawk
is the lord
of the sky.
Even the wind
pauses,
stands aside
when it passes
overhead.

In the Frozen

shallow water
of the ditch
along the road,
a deer skeleton,
smiling a long
smile of ribs, asked,
"What did I do
to deserve this?"
"You were born
a deer," I answered.

The Mississippi

is a pencil.
It is a pen.

It has been writing the story of water
since time immemorial.

It is the strip
of silver tape holding the ripped continent together.

It is the slick track
of the snail of the hemisphere.

It is the wick
of the oil lamp of the nation furiously burning out.

It is a bone, a shin bone.
It is a steel eel.

It is a stick.
It is a whip.

It is a divining rod.
It is a little history.

It is how America

takes a piss in the Gulf of Mexico.

Explanations

There are two ways
to explain why

the world
is so fucked up.

There is no god.
There are too many gods.

Hamlet Haiku

Hamlet

?????
???????
????!

The Ghost As It Appears to Gertrude In Act III Scene 4

Ophelia

(((((
(((())))
)))))

Claudius

11111
1111111
1111*

Gertrude

*0000
0000000
00000

Polonius

etc et
c etc etc
etc et

Horatio

I II III IV V

VI VII VIII IX X XI XII

XIII XIV XV XVI XVII

Rosencrantz

R&G R&
G R&G R&G
R&G R&

Guildenstern

R&G R&
G R&G R&G
R&G R&

Bullets

Michael M. came to my office. He had missed classes.
He's in the army, and they send him places. He came
to make up a missed paper. He was wounded in Iraq.
His unit was fighting in the cemetery in Fallujah.
They were behind headstones, firing and taking fire.
A bullet struck the headstone next to him. A chunk
of stone struck him in the back, breaking two ribs.
He said he missed the class before the last because he
got word that his best friend was killed in Iraq. He said
he missed the last class because he got word that his best
friend's brother killed himself in Iraq. He said it's lousy,
isn't it? He said it was a bullshit war. He said he knew that,
that it was a bullshit war. But he was reenlisting anyway.
He said the benefits were great, especially the money
for college. He said they were taking care of him. He said
they were paying all his medical. I didn't say anything.
I don't think it was a long time. It felt like a long time.
I just stared at his t-shirt. It felt like a long time. Then
I got up and found an empty desk for him to use. He came
to write the paper he missed. I told him to put it on my
desk when he was done. He said, *Yes, sir.* For the rest
of the day, all I could think about were bullets. The bullet
that sent a splinter of headstone into his back.

The bullet that pierced his best friend's heart. The bullet
that blew out his best friend's brother's brains. The bullet
I wanted to put through the words *Yes, sir*. The bullet
big enough to kill this bullshit bullshit bullshit war.

Poem with a Line by Antonio Porchia

He who tells the truth
says almost nothing.
And he who remains silent says
exactly what we want to hear.

New Journey

It cannot be a quest
because he would refuse
the hero's portion.

It cannot be a circle
because he would refuse
the returning.

It cannot be a river
because he would refuse
the drifting down.

It cannot be an ocean
because he would refuse
the counting of degrees.

It cannot be a mountain
because he would refuse
the leaving of the valley.

It cannot be a crossing
because he would refuse
the learning of the languages.

It cannot be a search

because he would refuse

the opening of the eyes.

Poem for Inclusion in My Will

When I die, I do not want to be buried.
I do not want to decompose, slowly, agonizingly,

like an old tree trunk, rotting and rotting and rotting away
season after season. I do not want to be buried.

I want to be burned. I want to be burned like the oak
that is struck by lightning in the storm, splintered,

scorched, charred. I want to be smoke and ashes.
I want to be smoke swirling upward in the air.

I want to be ashes blown by the wind over the river.
I do not want to be buried in the clodded earth,

the clay-suffocated earth. I want to be buried
in the air. I want to be breath. I want my transformation

swift, instantaneous, quick as a flash.
I want to dazzle like a magician's trick.

I want you left there to wonder:
How did he do that?

If You Should See Me Walking on the Road

If you should see me walking on the road
alone in the rain, without coat or covering,
my hair matted, the rain running like long
slender plaits of silver hair down my neck,
my shoulders, and I am not smiling, do not
be concerned. Do not worry, for I will know
where I am, and I will know where I am going.
But if you should see me walking on the road
alone in the rain, without coat or covering,
my hair matted, the rain running like long
slender plaits of silver hair down my neck,
my shoulders, and I am smiling, be concerned.
There will be reason to worry, for I will not know
where I am, and I will not know where I am going.

About the Author

J.R. Solonche is the author of *Beautiful Day* (Deerbrook Editions), *Won't Be Long* (Deerbrook Editions), *Heart's Content* (Five Oaks Press), *Invisible* (nominated for the Pulitzer Prize by Five Oaks Press), *The Black Birch* (Kelsay Books), *I, Emily Dickinson & Other Found Poems* (Deerbrook Editions), *In Short Order* (Kelsay Books), *Tomorrow, Today & Yesterday* (Deerbrook Editions), *True Enough* (Dos Madres Press), *The Time of Your Life* (forthcoming April 2020 from Adelaide Books), *The Porch Poems* (forthcoming 2020 from Deerbrook Editions), and coauthor of *Peach Girl: Poems for a Chinese Daughter* (Grayson Books). He lives in the Hudson Valley.